THE BIRTH OF MODERN TECH

AMERICAN ERAS: DEFINING MOMENTS

MARTIN GITLIN

CHERRY LAKE PRESS

Published in the United States of America by Cherry Lake Publishing Group
Ann Arbor, Michigan
www.cherrylakepublishing.com

Content Adviser: Kevin Whinnery, MA, History
Reading Adviser: Beth Walker Gambro, MS, Ed., Reading Consultant, Yorkville, IL
Photo Credits: © Science History Images/Alamy Stock Photo, cover, 1; © Maxiphoto/istock, 5;
   © Roland Magnusson/Shutterstock, 7; © aquatarkus/Shutterstock, 8; © Barry Lewis/Alamy Stock
   Photo, 9; © Hadrian/Shutterstock, 10; © ARPANET/Wikimedia, 13; © Adam "FastLizard4" Adam/
   Flickr, 14; © Leonard Zhukovsky/Shutterstock, 15; © Photo by Scott J. Ferrell/Library of Congress/
   LOC Control No. 2019643625, 16; © sung woo kim/Shutterstock, 19; © Maridav/Shutterstock, 20;
   © 2015 Larry D. Moore. Licensed under CC BY-SA 4.0, 21; © THINK A/Shutterstock, 22; © Gorodenkoff/
   Shutterstock, 25; © Gorodenkoff/Shutterstock, 26; © whiteMocca/Shutterstock, 28

Cherry Lake Press is an imprint of Cherry Lake Publishing Group.

Library of Congress Cataloging-in-Publication Data
Names: Gitlin, Marty, author.
Title: The birth of modern tech / by Martin Gitlin.
Description: Ann Arbor, Michigan : Cherry Lake Publishing, [2022] | Series: American eras: defining
   moments | Includes bibliographical references and index.
Identifiers: LCCN 2021007868 (print) | LCCN 2021007869 (ebook) | ISBN 9781534187436 (hardcover) |
   ISBN 9781534188839 (paperback) | ISBN 9781534190238 (pdf) | ISBN 9781534191631 (ebook)
Subjects: LCSH: Cell phone systems—United States—History—Juvenile literature. | Internet—History—
   Juvenile literature. | Internet of things—History—Juvenile literature. | Artificial intelligence—United
   States—History—Juvenile literature.
Classification: LCC TK5102.4 .G58 2022 (print) | LCC TK5102.4 (ebook) | DDC 004.0973—dc23
LC record available at https://lccn.loc.gov/2021007868
LC ebook record available at https://lccn.loc.gov/2021007869

Cherry Lake Publishing Group would like to acknowledge the work of the Partnership for 21st Century
Learning, a Network of Battelle for Kids. Please visit http://www.battelleforkids.org/networks/p21
for more information.

Printed in the United States of America
Corporate Graphics

ABOUT THE AUTHOR

Martin Gitlin has written more than 150 educational books. He also won more than 45 awards
during his 11-year career as a newspaper journalist. Gitlin lives in Cleveland, Ohio.

TABLE OF CONTENTS

The year was 1968. Paul Baran had a tough task in front of him. He worked for the RAND Corporation. This nonprofit company performs research for the U.S. military.

Baran was trying to figure out a way for people to share computers remotely. Small desktop and laptop computers were still years away from reality. So he launched a network that could be used by other scientists and researchers.

His invention allowed military personnel to communicate after a nuclear attack. It was successfully tested. Little did Baran know that his invention would lead to the creation of the internet.

Baran wasn't alone in paving a path to the future. Among the others were Robert Noyce and Gordon Moore. They started a **semiconductor** company called Intel. Their work made it possible for the **innovation** of personal computers. They also helped make the internet a reality.

Experts also consider Alan Turing, a British mathematician, to be the "father of modern computer science."

The work of scientists in the 1950s and 1960s changed the world forever. Their research led to technology that continues to expand and be explored. It has led to advances that make life easier and more enjoyable for people. The birth of the internet was perhaps the most important. But it was not the first.

CHAPTER 1

The Cell Phone

Modern communication didn't start with the internet. One can argue that it began with the cell phone. This invention allowed people to communicate anywhere. It affected everything, from people's personal lives to their workplace to the businesses they interacted with.

It all started on April 3, 1973. That's when Dr. Martin Cooper made the first mobile phone call. The Motorola employee called a friend who worked for the rival company AT&T. The phone

Dr. Martin Cooper made the first cell phone call while walking the streets of New York City, New York.

weighed more than 2 pounds (0.9 kilograms) and took 10 hours to charge. Back then, "mobile" phones were limited to car phones. These expensive phones cost thousands of dollars to install in cars and included more than 30 pounds (13.6 kg) of special equipment.

The first cell phone was limited to 35 minutes
of talk time before needing to be charged.

Early cell phones were primarily marketed for work and not personal use.

Motorola continued to work on cell phone technology. It finally made one for public use in 1983. But it was far too expensive for most people. The phone cost a whopping $4,000!

Cell phone **manufacturers** continued to expand services. Japanese cell phone company Sharp introduced the first camera phone in 2000. The phones became available in the United States 2 years later.

Early cell phones did not have the capability to send or receive text messages until Nokia, an electronics company, introduced a phone capable of doing this in 1993.

About 60 percent of adults in the United States owned cell phones by 2004. That number rose to 96 percent by 2016.

By then, most Americans had gone beyond that technology. Apple Computer founder Steve Jobs released the first iPhone in 2007. It allowed users to use the internet on their phones. More than half of American adults owned smartphones by 2014. Nearly 75 percent were using them in 2018.

The ability to connect to the internet through cell phones changed online technology forever. But it was the creation of the internet itself that made it all possible.

The First Mobile Game

Kids and adults have enjoyed playing games since the beginning of time. Mobile phones provided a new outlet in 1994. That is when the Hagenuk MT-2000 installed a version of the popular arcade game *Tetris*. The launching of the game *Snake* on the Nokia 6110 helped the mobile gaming industry take off. *Snake* gained popularity because it was simple to play, and people of all ages enjoyed it. *Snake* continues to be a popular game with hundreds of different versions. What modern game today do you think is an equivalent to *Snake*? Do you think that game will still be popular decades later? Why or why not?

CHAPTER 2

The Internet

Communication scientists who built the foundation for the internet couldn't have imagined its impact on American society. During the late 1960s, the Advanced Research Projects Agency Network (ARPANET) was created and funded by the U.S. Department of Defense. It was originally designed to send coded messages between two **terminals**. Those messages would then be **deciphered** by code experts. ARPANET laid the foundation for the internet we know today. The first communicated message happened on October 29, 1969, between two computers at separate universities: Stanford University and the University of California, Los Angeles.

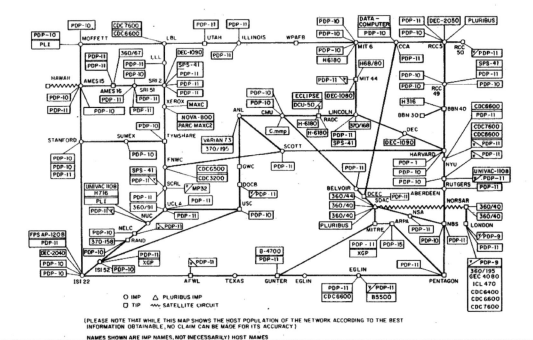

ARPANET LOGICAL MAP, MARCH 1977

The internet was initially a military project. The United States was afraid of an attack that would cut off vital communication.

Universities and research centers began to use this simplified version of the internet during the 1970s and 1980s. Some public and private businesses also joined the network. They mainly used this network for email, which was invented by Ray Tomlinson in 1971. It wasn't until Tim Berners-Lee invented the World Wide Web in 1989 that the internet took its current modern form. Soon, it was the largest computer network in the world. Already during the 1980s and 1990s, this computer network boasted 4 million systems and 70 million users.

The first message sent over the internet was supposed to read "Login," but only the first two letters were successfully sent. Pictured is the SDS Sigma-7, the first computer to send a message.

The explosion had just begun. Nearly 300 million Americans had internet access by the year 2020. It had radically altered the way almost everyone lived.

The internet changed the way Americans communicated. It changed how they shopped and got their news. It changed how they learned and were entertained. It changed how they worked and how they played.

Many investors were overly enthusiastic about the internet and invested money in early internet companies. Unfortunately, this enthusiasm caused the "dot-com" bubble.

At the turn of the century, also referred to as Y2K, everyone was in a panic, believing computers, the internet, and technology would have a difficult time transitioning from 1999 to 2000. Pictured is the President's Council on the Year 2000 Conversion news conference.

It even changed relationships between friends and strangers. The internet led to social media outlets such as Facebook, Twitter, and Instagram. It allowed Americans to connect with people all over the world. It created a platform for people to express their opinions.

Americans spend hours each day on the internet. The result isn't always positive. It has often meant less personal time with family and friends. Some believe the art of conversation has been lost. Disagreements about issues on social media have led to angry posts and even violence.

The internet created both positive and negative results. The goal among most Americans is to work to make it a more positive force for good in the future. Connecting the internet to devices inside and outside the home certainly makes life easier for people.

From 1G to 5G

Wireless technology has allowed Americans to connect to the world. The advancements over the years have been in speed and how far their signals can reach. People began using the internet through their dial-up phones at home. The technology has come a long way since then. It's reached a peak with the 5G mobile network. It allows users to connect reliably not only to other people, but also to machines, objects, and devices. However, that involves some controversy. Some people fear that 5G might affect human health. With almost every technological advancement, there seems to be pushback and fear. Why do you think that is?

CHAPTER 3

The Internet of Things

In 1999, Kevin Ashton coined a term that would become famous. Ashton worked at huge American manufacturer Proctor & Gamble. He helped supply products to be sold to **consumers**.

Ashton had learned that it was possible to place **sensors** in physical objects that would link them to the internet. He told his colleagues about it, calling it the "Internet of Things."

The new technology didn't take off for another decade. But by 2014, the Internet of Things (IoT) was beginning to make life easier for many Americans. It was helping them in their daily lives.

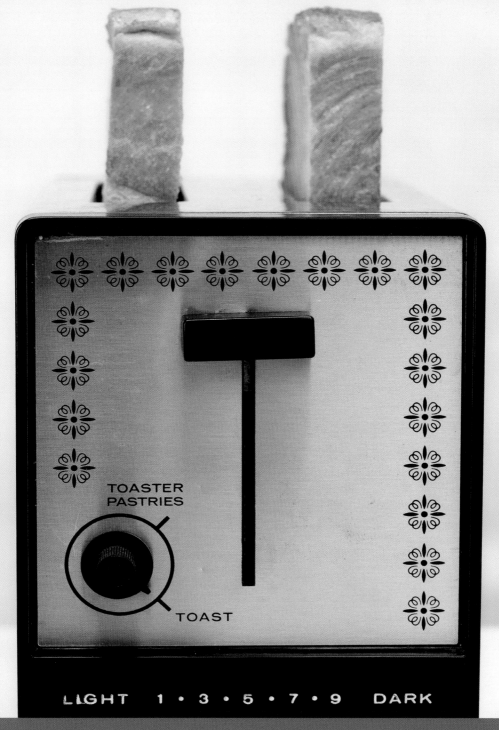

LIGHT 1 • 3 • 5 • 7 • 9 DARK

Some say the first IoT device can be traced back to
a "smart toaster" invented by John Romkey in 1990.

Connected devices make everyday life easier
by automating tasks and chores.

The possibilities seemed endless. Connected wearables like Fitbits let people know how many miles they walk or minutes they exercise. Home sensors allow people to turn on the oven or lights while driving home from work. IoT made it possible to create self-driving cars. Farmers could run their machinery without lifting a finger.

The term "Internet of Things" was coined by Kevin Ashton in 1999 during a presentation.

Experts believe that by 2025, 75 billion devices will be connected to the internet!

The new technology also helps entire towns and cities. Hooking up the internet to garbage cans lets collectors know that they're ready for pickup. Placing sensors in streetlights can help traffic move smoother and faster.

Some have criticized IoT. They feel it makes people far less mobile. They ask why it's necessary to lock a door remotely rather than get up and do it **manually**. But connected devices that help people exercise and save time have countered that argument.

People have waged the same debate about other new technologies. One of them is **artificial** intelligence.

Big Data and the Three V's

The term "big **data**" refers to facts so numerous or complex that it's difficult to process using traditional methods. Analyst Doug Laney worked on the idea of accessing and storing big data in the early 2000s. He created a new definition of big data as volume, velocity, and variety. Volume is the storage of data on cheaper platforms. Velocity results in faster **streaming** of data due to the use of IoT technology. Variety places data into a wide range of formats. Included are text documents, emails, and videos.

Artificial Intelligence

Stanford University computer scientist John McCarthy founded a field of study in 1955. He called it artificial intelligence (AI). It's the ability of a computer program or machine to think and learn. AI allows machines or programs to mimic human **cognition**.

The concept took a step forward in 1956. That is when researchers at Dartmouth College in New Hampshire wrote programs considered incredible at the time. These programs are simple by today's standards. They showed how AI could be used to solve word problems or beat people in checkers.

Between 1957 and 1974, computers were increasingly becoming more sophisticated, laying the framework for AI to flourish.

AI also helps collect, sort, and process all the data and information that is uploaded onto the internet.

Television shows and movies had been showing forms of AI for many years. One example was robots that were programmed to think like people and do work for them.

The creation of newer and faster computers resulted in $1 billion spent on AI research by 1985. New computer programs used in the fields of medicine and data collection triggered even more focus on AI and its potential.

The goal of AI scientists has been to solve problems in many areas. AI involves a wide range of fields, including computer science, math, medicine, and psychology.

Technology has rapidly developed since the invention of the internet.

Research & Act

Modern technology encompasses so many inventions and advances. Included are cell phones, personal computers leading to the internet, artificial intelligence (AI), and the **blockchain**. Is it too early to determine which of these and others will make the biggest impact on people around the world? Research all the different modern technologies and draw a conclusion for yourself. Discuss your findings with a family member or friend.

Timeline

1936: Alan Turing publishes a paper that leads to the foundation of computer science.

1950: Alan Turing develops the Turing test that determines whether a machine can be detected as a machine or pass as a human. This leads to the basis of AI.

1955: Stanford University researcher John McCarthy founds the field of Artificial Intelligence.

1968: RAND employee Paul Baran creates the first internet network.

October 29, 1969: ARPANET sends the first message from one computer at UCLA to another at Stanford University.

April 3, 1973: Motorola employee Martin Cooper makes the first cell phone call.

1976: Apple founders Steve Jobs and Steve Wozniak launch the first personal home computer.

1989: British scientist Tim Berners-Lee invents the World Wide Web, which is later known as Web 1.0.

1994: Mobile gaming is launched with *Tetris* on the Hagenuk MT-2000.

1997: The mobile gaming industry takes off with the release of *Snake* on the Nokia 6110.

1999: Proctor and Gamble employee Kevin Ashton coins the term "Internet of Things" (IoT).

2001: Apple releases the iPod MP3 player, revolutionizing music listening.

October 2004: Web 2.0 is coined by O'Reilly Media to describe the rise in content creation, such as social media and blogs, using the internet.

2007: Apple introduces the iPhone.

2020s: Experts believe that the internet is undergoing yet another evolution. Web 3.0 could potentially consist of emerging technologies like the blockchain and the Internet of Everything (IoE).

Further Research

BOOKS

Gitlin, Martin. *Smart Homes*. Ann Arbor, MI: Cherry Lake Publishing, 2021.

Gregory, Josh. *Steve Jobs*. New York, NY: Children's Press, 2013.

Johnson, Bryan R. *The Proto Project: A Sci-Fi Adventure of the Mind for Kids Ages 9–12*. New York, NY: Candy Wrapper, 2019.

WEBSITES

Britannica Kids: Technology and Invention
https://kids.britannica.com/kids/article/Technology-and-Invention/353296

Ducksters—Internet Safety
https://www.ducksters.com/internetsafety.php

Glossary

artificial (ar-tih-FISH-uhl) not real or genuine

blockchain (BLAHK-chayn) a digital ledger, or list of information, that records exchanges or interactions between different parties

cognition (kahg-NIH-shuhn) activities of thinking, understanding, and learning

consumers (kuhn-SOO-muhrz) people who buy and use products and services

data (DAY-tuh) facts that can be used in calculating, reasoning, or planning

deciphered (dee-SY-fuhrd) found the hidden meaning of something

innovation (ih-nuh-VAY-shuhn) new idea, device, or method

manually (MAN-yoo-wuh-lee) done in person or by hand

manufacturers (man-yuh-FAK-chuhr-uhrz) companies that make products

semiconductor (seh-mee-kuhn-DUHK-tuhr) material or object that allows electricity or heat to move through it

sensors (SEN-suhrz) devices that detect heat, light, sound, or motion

streaming (STREE-ming) playing continuously as data is sent to a computer over the internet

terminals (TUHR-muh-nuhls) computer screens and keyboards used to send commands to other computers

INDEX